Light of My Life,

Love on Your Journey

A Pet Storybook

A message story for a pet before, during or after a death transition.

Written and Illustrated by

L. Leigh Love

Bridge-of-Light Publishing™

Illustrated by L. Leigh Love

ISBN: 979-8-9895274-3-4 (hardcover)
ISBN: 979-8-9895274-4-1 (paperback)
ISBN: 979-8-9895274-6-5 (ebook)

Dedicated to my sweet Mattie,
and a shared love of ours, J.K.

And to all great loves.

Table of Contents

Preface

I wrote this more than a year and a half after my sweet Mattie died. She was a senior girl who got cancer. During the last portion of her life she was very sick. We managed the best we could, but we both knew what was to come. It was very hard on a daily basis. Death is never easy. When it happens suddenly, you are in shock. When it happens slowly, you don't know what to do or how to manage. Both can be paralyzing.

For almost fifteen years, Mattie was with me and I felt so very loved being with her. She taught me the value of family and true partnership. I miss her loving presence in my life. We had a soul-to-soul connection which I knew spanned lifetimes. There are some beings who are just meant to be together.

While in many ways it is fortunate to have a long good-bye, you still never know when that time will come. I wanted to be strong for her and to help her on her journey. I also wanted, and needed, to tell her things at the end of her life. I just didn't know what to say or how to say them. And, I wanted most of all, for her to feel loved.

Mattie once asked, in an animal communication session, for me to read to her. What a lovely request this was. Even though she is no longer with me in the physical, I wrote this story for her and I read it to her often. I know love transcends time and a part of her hears it.

I also wrote this story for others who might feel the same about their beloved pet and want, or need, an expression of love and honoring for their pet around the end of their life. It gives me great peace, courage, connection, and healing. I hope it provides the same for you.

— L. Leigh Love

Introduction

'Light of My Life, Love on Your Journey' is a different style of storybook. It was created and designed to help around end-of-life times of a beloved pet or animal companion. It is also here to help in the grief healing process of pet loss.

The **Preface** provides some background of why this storybook was created and how it evolved. The **Introduction** section, here, outlines the scope of content and ideas for use. Other sections of this book include the **Pet Message Story, Author Notes,** and **Shared Experiences.** Below are the descriptions of each section in the book.

'Light of My Life, Love on Your Journey' Pet Message Story

The story is here to provide a structure for giving a message to a beloved pet before, during, or even after an end-of-life transition. Death is a tough transition to manage and it is often hard to know what to do or to say during this time. There are a lot of emotions to process. Each verse section of the story holds a specific energy and meaning.

Listed below are some thoughts and ideas on when and how the pet message story can be used. It can be read completely and thoroughly as is, or it also can be tailored, as desired. The story can be read once or re-read many times. Grief is a process with many layers. You may find the themes in various sections resonate more at different times or that certain themes repeat for a while. Take as much time as needed with each section.

There are many moments in which the story can be used. This can be before, during or even after an end-of-life transition. Here are some of some thoughts and ideas on each.

Before an End-of-Life Transition

In the times before an end-of-life transition, such as senior years or chronic illness, this story can provide a message of love and preparation emotionally of what is to come. It can be used to create space for shared moments of a deep and profound connection of expressing love, honoring, and gratitude with your beloved pet.

End-of-life times are often hard to face. But taking time to talk about it and share messages of what you want your beloved pet to know can be invaluable. It can provide a soothing, soul-settling experience, as well as great peace and healing.

The pet message story can be read one-on-one with your pet. It can be a fantastic intimate expression and experience with them. It can be read with others or together as a family, and can help adults and children alike. It can also be read alone and privately to them in your heart.

So often we need, or wish we had had, a way to let our pet or animal companion know what they meant to us and what we wish for them. Animals innately feel our intentions and emotions. It is how they connect with us. We know they hear us. And taking a dedicated time, in a special and meaningful way, enhances this. Sharing this story or a message with our beloved pet, while they are here with us in the physical, is a great and glorious gift. This message story is here to help provide that.

During an End-of-Life Transition

When the opportunity is there, the pet message story can be helpful during the actual time of an end-of-life transition. Sometimes, we are in a position of being able to be present and attend to a peaceful transition of our beloved pet or animal companion.

Inherently, we know the transition of a soul is sacred. In the delicate and tender moments of death, we often feel there should be more, and something heartfelt on the soul level. And when it is not there, it feels empty and missing. This void can linger and cause much angst. The **'Light of My Life, Love on Your Journey'** pet message story can be read to your pet during this time to help provide loving energy, support and connection.

After an End-of-Life Transition

The beauty of the soul and sharing a heart-to-heart connection is that the love is always there. Love transcends time and space. And love exists in its own realm. So, this message story can be used for any love, anywhere and at any time. This includes after, or even long after, a death occurred. If you did not get the opportunity to have shared a message with your beloved pet while they were in the physical, it can still be done. And doing so is simple.

To do this, just take a special, dedicated time and say their name or hold an image of your beloved pet in your heart. You can use a picture of them or create a special honoring space, if you like. When you are ready, then read the story to them aloud or in your heart. The message conveys on the soul-to-soul, and heart-to-heart level and is felt deeply. Sometimes, we just need an expression of love, thanks, and honoring to our beloved pet to settle our soul and help give us peace during this tender time.

Author Notes

This work is about managing the death transition of a beloved pet who touched your life deeply. It is also about the transformation of healing grief. The **Author Notes** section provides further discussion and review of the energy and intention held with each verse of the story. It is here for those who wish for a greater understanding and exploration of the sections of the pet message story. Sometimes, this helps bring the meaning closer to our heart and creates a deeper, more elevated expression and experience. This also can allow us to explore on a deeper level what each of the verse intimately and uniquely means to us and our pet relationship. Take as much time as needed with this section.

Shared Experiences

So often we feel alone with our grief. This section contains some brief stories and reflections about others experiences with the storybook and healing from their pet's death transition. These are included to provide comfort in sharing during this tender time and a simple reminder that there are others out there who 'get it' and have deep and loving relationships with their pets. This section is here to help you know you are not alone.

'Light of My Life, Love on Your Journey' pet message story, provides a guiding structure for managing many aspects of the death of a loving relationship. It was written with a true understanding of how difficult this time is and how important it is to have an expression of love and honoring. Reading the message story can also be a way to re-connect to the relationship and the love shared.

The correct way to use this book is however you want. Use the message story as you see fit and take only that which what feels right. Allow any and or all parts of this storybook to be a bridge to healing and a connection back to the love shared.

The **'Light of My Life, Love on Your Journey'** pet message story is a soul-to-soul expression of love. It is also a gift to the recipient. Love and honoring are the greatest gifts we can give.

Light of My Life,
Love on Your Journey

Story

There was once a great love.

It was between you and me.

It started in our hearts,
For everyone to see.
And here it will remain,
For all of eternity.

A journey we took,
A life we shared.
Two hearts together,
A love we dared.

Sometimes it was rough,
Most times it was grand.
You and me together,
Hand-in-hand.

Light of my life, love on your journey.

Memories abound,
Are tried and true.
I hold these glorious thoughts,
And I honor you.

All parties must end,
And I want you to know,
I'd do it all over again,
And I love you so.

Light of my life, love on your journey.

At this tough time,
When we must part,
We both know...
It's only in the physical,
And not of the heart.

Time draws near,
And curtains will close.
Though, the show is not over,
As love only grows.

You made life happier.
You made life whole.
You are my true family,
And I love your soul.

Light of my life, love on your journey.

Light shining down,
From the heavens above,
Inviting Angels,
To bless and be with you.

A moment of reverence in asking,
God's grace and shining glory,
To surround you with love,
And to bless our story.

Light of my life, love on your journey.

It will be hard,
But for you I will be brave.
I am forever grateful,
For all that you are,
And all that you gave.

Let's be in the moment of love,
And hold peace of mind.
Shine bright, my dear,
Our hearts are forever entwined.

Light of my life, love on your journey.

At this tender time, my promise is true.
I will be your bright star,
For no matter how long,
For no matter how far.

Through journeys of life,
Through journeys of death,
You will always be in,
My every breath.

Light of my life, love on your journey.

I adore you so much,
And I want you to know,
You are the light of my life,
And I love you so.

This will carry us forward,
For the future to be...

There is a great love.

It is between you and me.

Light of My Life,
Love on Your Journey

Author Notes

Here are additional notes for further review and discussion of the verses of the story. Each section is designed to hold a central message and energy. The story can assist in the process of transitioning through and healing grief. Certain sections may resonate more at different times. Themes may repeat. Take as much time as needed with each part.

The notes here can help bring meaning closer to the heart and create a deeper, more elevated experience and expression of love to your pet. This also can allow exploration of what each section intimately and uniquely means to us. One idea is to play around with the story verses and think about or write what each means for you and your pet. You can also use this as a guideline to create your own pet message story.

For further exploration, each verse is listed, and is followed by a discussion of the deeper meaning and energy.

There was once a great love.
It was between you and me.

The story opens and draws the listener in with a simple foundation statement of a beautiful love and who it was with. It is intimate and affectionate. Here, there is no doubt of the depth of love and connection between the reader and the listener. It also opens the door for exploring and setting the stage for this great love story.

It started in our hearts,
For everyone to see.
And here it will remain,
For all of eternity.

This phrase is a reminder that the connection is of the heart and it existed beautifully and fully expressed in the world. And, what a glorious thing it is. Love never dies. There is a beauty to a loving and deep relationship.

To quote John Keats,

> **"A thing of beauty is a joy for ever:**
> **Its loveliness increases; it will never**
> **Pass into nothingness..."**
> **—Endymion, John Keats**

The verse here is a reflection of this same sentiment, on all levels. Mr. Keats completely understood beauty and love to their core. My favorite part is that he reminds us that, not only is beauty (and love) everlasting, but that it increases. Just spend a moment fully grasping this, feel it within, and deeply know how true it really is. This alone can provide much needed comfort, inner peace, and healing.

A journey we took,
A life we shared.
Two hearts together,
A love we dared.

Here, is a reflective moment of the wonderful opportunity to have shared the experience of life and love together. And what a journey it was; a love we dared. It's not always widely accepted that deep love can exist between beings or even between different types of beings. This verse is an expression of daring to love beyond boundaries of all sorts and just being able to be in a pure connection on a soul-to-soul level with another. How glorious this is.

Sometimes it was rough,
Most times it was grand.
You and me together,
Hand-in-hand.

This verse is fully owning that there were difficult times and challenges. But, above it all, the love and true connection shined through. The phrase 'hand-in-hand' is a symbolic reflection of a great partnership. We often don't take time to realize how our pets partner with us in life. This is true of any great love.

Light of my life, love on your journey.

The core of this message story is summed up in these two parts, wanting your beloved to know they are the light of your life and sending love to them on their journey. It is worth repeating, over and over.

Memories abound,
Are tried and true.
I hold these glorious thoughts,
And I honor you.

The reflection here is on the abundant lifetime memories that are heartfelt, deep, solid, and brilliant. We hold these up and are called to acknowledge and honor the soul qualities and the contributions our beloved pet made to our life. To 'honor' is to recognize greatness. It lets our beloved, and the universe, know how much we recognize and appreciate them. An honoring is a blessing for the soul. Not only does honoring offer a gift to our pet, it helps create peace within because we are giving something back. Love and honoring are the greatest gifts we can give.

All parties must end,
And I want you to know,
I'd do it all over again,
And I love you so.

This simple statement reminds us that death is a part of life. Ted Andrews reflects on this further in his book, Animal Speak:

> **"There is no life without death and no death without rebirth."**
> **—Animal Speak, Ted Andrews**

What a lovely reminder this is. Included in this verse is also a statement to our beloved that we hold our time together in the highest regards. In these moments also, it seems we can't say, "I love you" enough. Our love for them is mentioned again, just to express this. Our soul needs to say this many, many times. And it feels so good to do so.

Light of my life,
Love on your journey.

The core of this message story is summed up in these two parts, wanting your beloved pet to know they are the light of your life and sending love to them on their journey. It is worth repeating, over and over. It reflects our awareness of their beauty and meaning in our life.

At this tough time,
When we must part,
We both know…
It's only in the physical,
And not of the heart.

This reflection helps remind us that, yes it will be tough, but while the physical fades, the love remains. It provides strength and refocus. Yes, it is hard to manage loss of a loved one in the physical; there is no doubt about that. It is a process. This section is here to help us keep our focus on the heart-love connection to our beloved within us.

Time draws near,
And curtains will close.
Though, the show is not over,
As love only grows.

Here, we are facing the inevitable and at the same time, we are aware that death does not end a relationship. Our love grows and deepens. And, if we allow it, there is an opportunity for us to reach beyond the physical. When we are ready, this section holds a gentle knowing that love exists in its own realm, which we can access anytime. This can bring us great comfort and joy.

You made life happier.
You made life whole.
You are my true family,
And I love your soul.

Simple facts and statements are made here of how our pet touched our life. We are letting them know the depth of their gifts, their contributions and how they greatly affected us. Also, this is a recognition of how family bonds are made of the heart and soul. Love is love and exists in its own realm. This provides a greater, broader perspective and understanding of the relationship shared and true family bond. It is a declaration of letting our beloved pet know how much we value them, and that this love is on the deepest level of our soul, that of family.

Light of my life, love on your journey.

The core of this message story is summed up in these two parts, wanting your beloved to know they are the light of your life and sending love to them on their journey. It is felt deeper every time we say it.

Light shining down,
From the heavens above,
Inviting Angels,
To bless and be with you.

Just a simple request, taking time to invite the loving support of angels and the divine to help guide your beloved safely home.

Let's take a moment to consider more about the act of blessing and honoring. There are many definitions and meanings of blessing. The word 'blessing' from the start evokes a sense of warmth, belonging, and protection. At its basic level, one definition of 'to bless' is to declare good, another is an 'invoking of or asking of God's favor'. In this verse, we are inviting the angels to bless our beloved pet. We are also participating in this blessing.

In John O'Donohue's book, '*To Bless the Space Between Us*', he reminds us that we all have the ability to bless. He encourages us to rediscover that we have the power to bless one another and states "Wherever one person takes another into the care of their heart, they have the power to bless." Just take a moment to realize how incredibly beautiful this really is.

A moment of reverence in asking,
God's grace and shining glory,
To surround you with love,
And to bless our story.

This is a private and special moment of asking God (or the Divine) to be with our beloved and provide them with comfort and care during this time. Included is also a request of the divine to shine through your life together, the challenges, the growth, the strength, and most of all...the love shared.

A blessing or honoring is a recognition of value and of greatness. It is an illumination. Blessings and honoring's are gifts. But, also know there is a divine connection between the two, the giver and the receiver, and there is a sacred intimate connection felt deep within.

Light of my life, love on your journey.

The core of this story message is summed up in these two parts, expressing to your beloved pet that they are the light of your life and sending love to them on their journey. It settles our soul. It brings us closer.

It will be hard, but for you I will be brave.
I am forever grateful,
For all that you are,
And all that you gave.

This section states what we may not want to face; knowing how difficult and painful it will be. But, we can be strong. We can strive to do this for ourselves and for our beloved pet. We can also invite them in to be with us and help guide our healing.

This verse also holds an expression of divine gratitude. It is letting our beloved pet know that we are so grateful they shared their life and their gifts with us. We are thanking them aloud, and in our hearts.

Let's be in the moment of love,
And hold peace of mind.
Shine bright, my dear,
Our hearts are forever entwined.

This section provides comfort and peace. After the tears are shed, this is a loving and gentle reminder of where to focus. Instead of the moment of loss, we can shift and reach higher to the energy of love and be in this space. It is also letting our beloved and ourselves be reminded that our souls are forever connected, forever entwined. And what a glorious and wonderful thing this is to truly know.

Light of my life, love on your journey.

The core of the message story is summed up in these two parts, wanting your beloved to know they bring you light and sending love to them on their journey. It is worth repeating for them...and us. It is also a reminder that your journey is my journey. It is our journey.

At this tender time, my promise is true.
I will be your bright star,
For no matter how long,
For no matter how far.

This verse holds the energy of support. It is acknowledging the tenderness of the moment and our commitment to shining our love for our beloved pet. A simple statement. A simple decree.

The hard part of not being the one who is dying, is being strong for the one who is, and for yourself. Making a statement helps. This is reminder that your love for them will always shine. Always.

Through journeys of life,
Through journeys of death,
You will always be in,
My every breath.

We have shared the complexities of life, and all of life, over and over again. This is letting our beloved pet know that, having shared this great love, it is now a part of me. We are saying to them that there is never a moment when you are not with me. You, my beloved, are a part of me now and forever.

I adore you so much.
And I want you to know,
You are the light of my life,
And I love you so.

This is a simple and honest statement straight from the heart. It is just another way to express our earnest feelings for our beloved. And it rings deep. Our heart overflows with adoration and love for them. It feels so good to express this. It brings us closer and it shines through everything.

This will carry us forward,
For the future to be.

This expression brings the loving energy of the relationship forward to the present. It also looks to the future knowing we will meet again and what a glorious reunion it will be.

There is a great love.
It is between you and me.

This is a powerful statement with the word 'is' being strategically placed. Note, the verb tense moved to the present, indicating, and reminding us of the strong existence of the love, pure and plain. This is a reminder that the love is still there and will continue to grow.

Light of my life,
Love on your journey.

Summary

This storybook was originally written for and inspired by the loss of a beloved pet. It is often not truly appreciated how deep and beautiful this relationship can be. But, 'love is love,' in all circumstances. And this story can apply to or be used in the honoring of **any** loved one or loving relationship, when a message is needed to be conveyed. Soul love does not differentiate. It can be read in-person with them or simply read to them privately, in your heart.

Death is an encounter we face many times, with many loved ones. We can have several great loves in our life, each as beautiful as the others. Every relationship is special, offering something unique to our lives and soul development. Each message and honoring to them will be different. When using this message story with a beloved, the colors and energy of the relationship will come through. Each section will hold unique meaning. At a different time, with a different beloved, the message story will enhance the feelings and specialness of that relationship. The messages, memories and meaning will evolve to encompass that specific relationship when read to them. The message story was written and designed to provide a structure by which the loved and honored relationship will shine through when read for a beloved.

Many blessings to you on your healing journey!

—*L. Leigh Love*

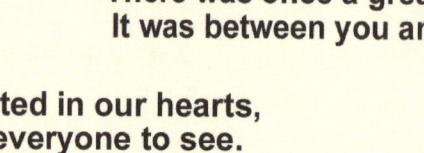

Light of My Life, Love on Your Journey

There was once a great love.
It was between you and me.

It started in our hearts,
For everyone to see.
And here it will remain,
For all of eternity.

A journey we took,
A life we shared.
Two hearts together,
A love we dared.

Sometimes it was rough,
Most times it was grand.
You and me together,
Hand-in-hand.

Light of my Life, Love on Your Journey.

Memories abound,
Are tried and true.
I hold these glorious thoughts,
And I honor you.

All parties must end,
And I want you to know,
I'd do it all over again,
And I love you so.

Light of my Life, Love on Your Journey.

At this tough time,
When we must part,
We both know...
It's only in the physical,
And not of the heart.

Time draws near,
And curtains will close.
Though, the show is not over,
As love only grows.

You made life happier.
You made life whole.
You are my true family,
And I love your soul.

Light of my Life, Love on Your Journey.

Light of My Life, Love on Your Journey

Light shining down,
From the heavens above,
Inviting Angels,
To bless and be with you.

A moment of reverence in asking,
God's grace and shining glory,
To surround you with love,
And to bless our story.

Light of my Life, Love on Your Journey.

It will be hard,
But for you I will be brave.
I am forever grateful for,
All that you are,
And all that you gave.

Let's be in the moment of love,
And hold peace of mind.
Shine bright, my dear,
Our hearts are forever entwined.

Light of my Life, Love on Your Journey.

At this tender time,
My promise is true.
I will be your bright star,
For no matter how long,
For no matter how far.

Through journeys of life,
Through journeys of death,
You will always be in,
My every breath.

Light of my Life, Love on Your Journey.

I adore you so much,
And I want you to know,
You are the light of my life,
And I love you so.

This will carry us forward,
For the future to be…

There is a great love,.
It is between you and me.

Light of My Life, Love on Your Journey.

-L. Leigh Love

33

Shared Experiences

Below are some stories from others and their experience with the storybook and healing their grief from pet loss. These are included to provide support and comfort in knowing you are not alone in feeling great love for your pet.

Peaceful Weight Lifted

*"I was so grateful to have had this story to read to my beloved, Blue, in his senior days. I knew it would be hard, but I took the time I needed with the book. And when I was ready, I read the story to him with my whole heart. And I'm so grateful I did. I know he heard me. It allowed us to have a conversation. This story was the bridge that allowed me to let him know all of the ways he helped me throughout my life and the through many difficult times of life. He was my rock...always there for me...so solid...so loving. I also let him know what I wished for him. We went for a nice walk afterwards, just the two of us. It was so settling. **I feel a weight lifted knowing what was in my heart was expressed to him.** This story provided the guidance to help me do that. When that time comes, his death transition will still be hard, no doubt, but I will have the peace of knowing we had this deep and profound shared connection and expression of thanks, honoring and blessings for his life and his being. I just may read it to him again."*

—Allison R., Seattle, Washington

Helpful anchor in healing

*"My cat, Xena Katrina, was the only one who understood me. I found her on the side of the road. She had been discarded. I rescued her, and she rescued me. Mostly, it's been just the two of us. I called her my warrior princess cat. She gave me courage, strength and love. Towards the end, she had kidney failure. The hospice vet helped evaluate quality of life and the 'when'. I read 'Light of My Life, Love on Your Journey' to her the few days prior. Once, Xena reached out her paw to my lips as if to say 'I know.' And 'thank you.' I read it to her again on the day of her last home vet visit. I got to express to her my eternal love and thankfulness. **It was a great anchor for me.** It's been hard without her, but I feel her with me. She comes to me in dreams and curls up on my lap with me reading to her."*

—Alex P., Charleston, SC

Continued Connection...

"I had a hard loss this year. Anyone who has deeply loved a pet can understand. I'm grieving the loss of a really special being, Orion. I called him 'a physical angel in a 'dog suit.' He touched my life in so many ways. He was my protector, way-shower and spread love everywhere he went! We are soul companions through and through. A special memorial was held to honor his soul and being. And I know he is still with me, just in a different form. 'Light of My Life, Love on Your Journey' gave me comfort. I read it to him a month after he passed. It helped me have ways to continue to express my love and honor for him. And it helped me keep our connection and to continue to feel and be aware of his presence around me. Regularly, when I'm on a walk, in our favorite place or out in nature, a butterfly will appear and my heart will enlighten with our love. Sometimes, it's a feather at my feet. I know it is Orion's being coming to say hi. I feel his presence and I am in gratitude for it. This has carried me through the grief on the wing of an angel, and that angel's name is Orion! **This book has helped me heal and find comfort in our continued relationship and unconditional love.**"

—DahVid W., Asheville, NC

Grateful family

"Jacob and Emma grew up with Buddy. He was always there with our family. Emma used to have tea parties with him. I'm still amazed he allowed her to dress him up. Jacob would play fetch with him in the yard for hours and even sometimes pretended to be a dog. Buddy would take turns sleeping with them. They traded every other night. And even though they said they didn't, I knew they were sneaking him food under the dinner table. As a parent, I was beside myself when Buddy could no longer walk. We were having to pick him up to go outside. I knew that time had come and my heart was breaking for our family. How are my children going to handle this? What can I do to help them manage his death? A friend suggested this book. I read through it first. And it was exactly what we needed. We took the time as a family and had our evening with Buddy. I'll be honest, it wasn't easy. But, Buddy deserved it and we needed it. We read the story to him and each took turn telling stories. We cried a lot. But, in the end we had our moment with him of saying goodbye and showing love for a beautiful life. We told him how much he meant to us. **Buddy was a part of our family and I can't imagine not having had this.**"

—Jamie J., Denver, CO

About the Author

(This is one of my favorite pictures. It was taken on one of our many beach trips together and snapped right before Mattie gave me a big sloppy kiss on the cheek.)

Author Bio: L. Leigh Love is an East Coast author and artist who very much enjoys connecting with nature and honoring all life...and the souls who enhance it. Her writing focuses on the inspirational and spiritual areas, with her artistic mediums being nature photography, digital art, acrylics, and alcohol ink. She is the author of the award-winning children's book, **'Roly-Poly and the Light' and 'A Pet Loss Comfort Book.'** She conducts Pet Honoring Memorial services and strives to continue to develop a variety of ways for us to honor our pets. **PetHonoring.com**

This book is Kelsey, Nimbo and Xander approved!

Kelsey - the inspiration for the **PetHonoring.com** work.
Nimbo - a soul companion in starting **4PawsFarewell** in Asheville, NC.
Xander - contributed to the energy and writing of this book.

Blessings and thanks to these beautiful beings!

Other Works by L. Leigh Love

'A Pet Loss Comfort Book & Grief Healing Toolbox', Fall 2024
A resource book for healing pet grief.

Pet Honoring DIY: Creating Your Own Pet Honoring Memorial Ceremony, 2025

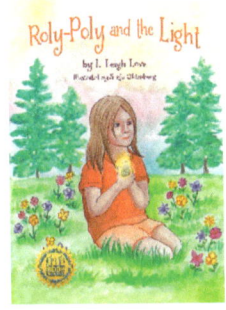

'Roly-Poly and the Light', 2023
Award-winning children's book about being different and the same.

'Max the Great', children's book about friendship, finding inner strength and overcoming obstacles. Coming 2026

LLeighLove.com

Bridge-of-Light Publishing™